Life in the Yorkshire Dales

A Pictorial Review

compiled by W. R. Mitchell

HORNBLOWER AT BAINBRIDGE

Dalesman Books

1980

The Dalesman Publishing Company, Ltd.,
Clapham (via Lancaster), North Yorkshire.

First published, 1980.

© Text, W. R. Mitchell, 1980.

ISBN: 085206 589 2

REETH BARTLE FAIR

Printed in Great Britain by Fretwell & Brian Ltd.,
Howden Hall, Howden Road, Silsden, Nr. Keighley, West Yorkshire.

Contents

*Front cover: Haytime in
Deepdale, near Dent.*

DONKEY WITH MILK CANS, CASTLE BOLTON

The Dales
in Pictures

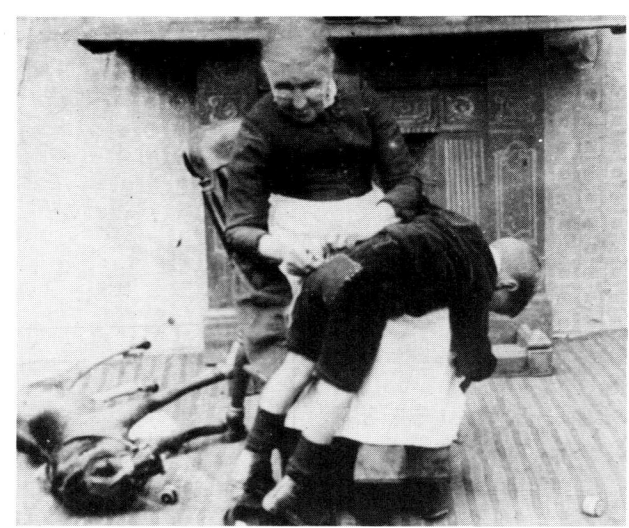

"NOWT'S T'SAME," said the Dales farmer, wistfully. His memory spanned the years of this century; he had been born, reared and married in the same small valley in the shadow of the Pennine ridges. He conceded that the appearance of the fells had not changed much — yet. He marvelled at the changing way of life.

He had mown meadows by scythe and driven cattle to market over many a weary mile. He had lived in terrible isolation at his dalehead holding. Those were the days before the telephone, radio and television had arrived to break down the seclusion of the Dales. He remembered "scrattin' for a livin'". There was never any spare money. When he went to school, "mam wrapped up some jam an' bread an' sad cakes for t'mid-day meal. If I felt thirsty after eating yon lot, I went across t'skooil yard an' had a sup o' cowd watter from a tap."

A person does not need to be ancient to recall the old ways, as this collection of photographs — submitted to *The Dalesman* between 1939 and 1979 — plainly indicates. The pictures have been selected to show distinctive aspects of the Dales way of life. Some pictures are old; others were taken the day-before-yesterday. All of them charm us by their quaintness.

The first photographers in the Dales needed a handcart for their equipment. Among them was Anthony Horner, of Settle, who was operating in the 1870s. He took with him a bulky camera and a small tent on a tripod which was his portable darkroom. He used the wet plate process. Each plate had to be sensitised on the spot, exposed and developed before it went dry.

Few "action" shots were attempted. The cameras were cumbersome, and many lacked shutters. One removed the lens cap for an exposure of several seconds, for the emulsion on a photographic plate was "slow." When I chatted with Frederic Riley, who wrote about North Craven and took many photographs, he remembered when, as a boy, he had his photograph taken. It was a dull day, and in the studio his head was firmly held in a clamp so that he could not move during the long exposure!

Few of the pictures in this collection date back to Victorian days. (That theme might be expanded in another book). My concern was to convey the vitality of Dales life, concentrating on dalesfolk at work. Those who wield the small, automatic cameras of today — and who continue the tradition of recording Dales life pictorially — have enormous advantages over the older generations, yet some pictures taken 60 or 70 years ago impress us as minor works of art. The old-time photographers were not snap-happy; they took time to compose their pictures.

A favourite photographer of the Dales scene and its people is Bertram Unne, who for many years operated from Harrogate. His fine collection of pictures now forms part of the archives of North Yorkshire. Another exponent with a quick eye for a lively Dales picture, and who is fond of portraying dalesfolk, is Geoffrey N. Wright; he now lives in Wensleydale. One might also pay tribute to the work of the late R. B. Fawcett, of Leyburn. Though best-known as an energetic journalist, he always carried a camera and his photography has helped to record Dales life during a period of rapid change.

This collection of prints concentrates on everyday life in the area that has become the Yorkshire Dales National Park. The area extends from Swaledale to Wharfedale, and from North Ribblesdale to Nidderdale (the last-named valley was unaccountably left out of the Park).

It is offered as an unpretentious record of life in the days before the machines took over, and before businessmen in town began to provide the goods and services which once were made and sustained in the dale country itself.

Acknowledgements

THE ILLUSTRATIONS in this book were from the following. The position of photographs on a page is indicated by letters – t for top, b for bottom, l for left and r for right.

G. H. Hesketh, 48 (bl), 58 (t); C. H. Wood, 66 (b); J. Handley, 59 (bl), 72 (tr); Werner Kissling, 70 (b), 73; Harry Metcalfe, 70 (r); Earby Mining Museum, 61 (b); Robert T. Clough, 59 (r); Craven Museum, 55 (b); R. Burton, 44 (l); F. O. Stead, 36 (l); F. H. Wright, 42 (t); Geoffrey N. Wright – front cover picture, 11 (r), 50, 54, 95, 96, 71 (tr); H. Lefevre, 48 (t), 74 (l); J. Dickinson, 35 (l); Shepherd and Walker collection – back cover picture; P. Walshaw, 26 (b), 33 (r), 48 (br); R. B. Fawcett – title page illustration, 3, 28, 40 (r), 59 (l), 79 (t), 80; Hubert Simpson, 39 (b); C. J. S. Atkinson, 16 (l); Mary Boothman, 30 (t), 53 (tr), 55 (t); F. Gegg, 2; G. Crowther, 31, 61 (r); Collection of Ronald Harker, 4; Collection of David Joy, 26 (t), 33 (b), 63, 65 (b), 66 (t); Wilfred Moore, 39 (tl); Bertram Unne, 6, 7 (tl), 9, 18 (l), 22, 23 (r), 24, 27, 35 (tr), 37, 44 (r), 46, 47, 72 (l), 75; John Snowden, 7 (tl); Ian Meiklejohn, 36 (r); John Fawcett, 8; Horner Collection, 38 (t), 62 (r), 64 (b), 65 (t), 78; J. Newton, 10; Miss M. A. Brown, 39 (tr); J. A. Carpenter, 11 (l), 61 (t); J. M. Capes, 41; W. R. Mitchell, 12, 13 (l), 16 (r), 17 (r), 18 (r), 31, 29 (r), 34 (r), 35 (b), 40 (l), 43 (t), 43 (bl), 55 (r), 58 (b), 60, 67 (l), 68, 69, 70 (t), 71 (tl), 71 (br), 74 (r); G. G. Hoare, 13 (r), 72 (b); Reece Winstone, 25; Ron and Lucie Hinson, 14 (t), 15, 32 (l), 38 (b), 45; H. Wade, 43 (br); W. Hubert Foster, 19; Overend Press, 42 (b), 49. A. Knowles-Fitton, 63 (t); John E. Kilburn, 63 (b).

The fell shepherd (portrayed on this page) typifies the hardy dale stock. He is sometimes taunted with the expression "dog and stick farmer". That stick is like an extra leg as he negotiates the steep fellsides; and it flashes with the speed of an adder's tongue to help him catch a recalcitrant ewe or a lamb which is normally "wick" enough to evade capture. The condition of the land and the climate has bred in the hill farmer a strong realism. He spends much time in his own company, and tends to be taciturn. His favourite time is when tewit and curlew return—when "t'back 'o winter's brokken." For the worst winters come near to breaking him.

Until the outbreak of the 1914-18 war, dalesfolk were almost a race apart — separated from the world by the lean Pennine ridges, by their own disinterest in what was happening outside the dale, and by their lack of mobility. For many, the local market town was the end of the road. They followed the way of life of a pastoral community, and much of the sheep-tending routine was little changed over 1,000 years, having affinities with that practised by the Norse folk.

Until Victoria's reign, not many people arrived in the Dales for pleasure. Towards the end of the century, the long isolation of the dalesfolk was ending. Today, thousands of visitors throng the Dales on a sunny day in summer...

Dalesfolk

UNTIL RECENT TIMES, life in the Yorkshire Dales was, for ordinary folk, a relentless tussle with the land and climate. There was little spare time, and no spare money. The land consists of thin soils and much outcropping rock. The climate is generally cool and cloudy, offering a short growing season and an almost unbearably long winter. Most of the dalesfolk emerge from the gruelling conditions with their spirits intact. They are, indeed, a bright-spirited folk, with a ready wit.

Above: Men of Bishopdale; a photograph taken at Thoralby. *Below:* A Swaledale farmer; Charles Alderson, of Muker. *Right:* Daleswoman; Mrs. B. Simpson, of Summerbridge.

Where Lean Lands Rake the Sky

Pennine horizons tend to be low — and bleak. On the left is a study of haytimers near Thwaite, in upper Swaledale. The men are using long-poled scythes. Cotterdale, pictured below, shows the narrow road extending between river and fell.

LOOK AT A MAP of the Dales, and you will be astonished at the large areas of little-known country that lie between the familiar dales. In the west, limestone obtrudes, as in our study (left) of farm stock grouped in a high pasture, with the summit of Ingleborough breaking the skyline. Notice that the cattle are horned (de-horning is now the rule). Limestone country offers sweet grazing for stock.

The term "fell", for a high hill, is from the Old Norse (*fjell* in Norway). The snowscape (right) is of Widdale, between Ingleton and Hawes. Notice how the walls, made without a dab of mortar, accentuate the contours of the fells, the sides of which sweep grandly up from the comparatively narrow stretch of good land. In this type of countryside, Norse names proliferate. Apart from fell, there is beck (a stream), gill (a water-carved valley), moss, heath and ling.

A farmer with a horse (far right) follows an old lane between drystone walls as he returns to a farm that is tucked away from the sight of the world near Bainbridge, in Wensleydale. In this dale, where the Yoredale series of rocks are conspicuous, many of the felltops look horizontal, as though they had been laid out by someone using a spirit level.

The types of land found in the upper dales are meadow (yielding grass for the annual hay crop, the winter fodder for the stock), pasture, rough grazing and open moor. On some moors, grazing is regulated by apportioning a certain number of stints to each local farm (a "stint" represents the pasturage of a single sheep). The stint is said to be governed by the number of sheep that can be wintered on the in-bye (or lower) land during the days when the moorland grazings are closed.

Sheep in View

DISTINCTIVE TYPES of sheep are needed for the high, exposed grazings of the Dales. That on the right is the Dalesbred sheep (notice the white flash on either side of the nostril), which is found mainly in Craven. The Swaledale sheep (pictured below) were photographed on a farm at the head of Ribblesdale. Dales farmers deal nimbly and firmly with the sheep, as shown by the farmer at Whaw, in Arkengarthdale (right) and the men who are hand-clipping above Muker, Swaledale.

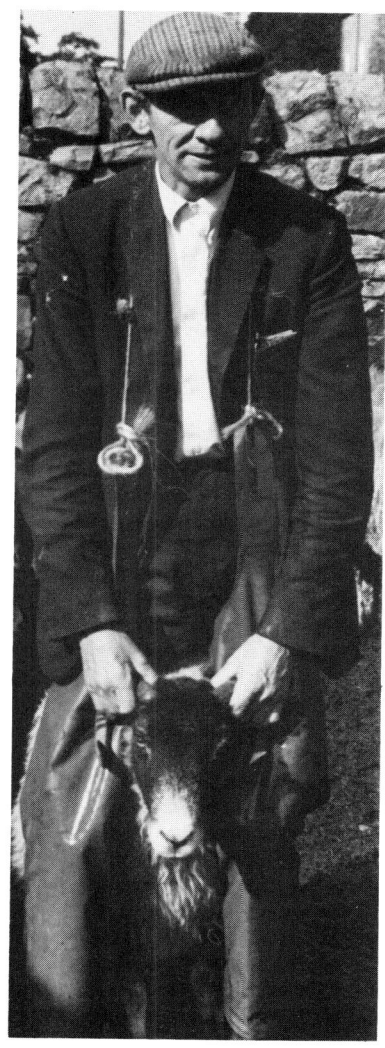

Sheep as passengers (left) were photographed on a moorland road between Wensleydale and Swaledale. A cattle wagon disgorges a travel-weary flock at Malham (below, left). An experienced farmer soon appraises the quality of sheep at Malham (below), and men stir into brisk life some of the animals mustered for a sale at Hawes auction mart (right).

Dales Faces

THERE IS NO SPECIFIC Dales face, but this little group of dalesmen is unified by the old-time fashion for growing a bushy moustache. Lines of merriment crease the face of the farmer (left), while an expression of concentration is noted (below) as a farmer carries hay to his sheep near Stainforth, in North Ribblesdale.

Thomas White, pictured above, was a quarryman employed at Beecroft, Horton-in-Ribblesdale. The farmer (far right) was on hill land at the rim of the Washburn Valley.

Life at Home

APPLYING A FRESH coat of whitening to the face of the farmhouse kept the family of Joseph Raw, Inghead, Garsdale, very busy during one of the long summer days (left). Hand-knitting, being demonstrated above, was a primary occupation at homes in the vicinity of Dent. Changes in fashion and attitudes is apparent in the closely-knit group (pictured right); this family living at Bell Busk, in Craven. There was a richness in family life in the days of the village school and meagre transport, which kept many families near home.

Village Shop

WE REMEMBER the bell that jangled — for minutes it seemed — just above the door as we entered the shop. In the days before pre-packaged food was the rule, we had our nostrils tickled by a delicious blend of dozens of odours from commodities being offered for sale. Their variety, and their random storage, bewildered us.

The Dales village shop was always something more than a mere retail outlet for household goods. There was personal service, and for every purchase there was an item of local gossip, offered entirely free. If a queue developed, no one fretted. Here was a chance to chat with the neighbours and friends.

We could buy anything from pins to patent medicines. When a commodity was being served loose, we watched entranced as the shop-keeper made a neat cone of paper. A similar cone held the few precious sweets over the purchase of which a small child might deliberate for half an hour

The old photograph (left) of Litton Post Office in the days when mail was transported by horse and carriage shows that H. Battersby was a tailor, who held a licence to sell tobacco. The sub postmaster in the Dales might also serve as a weather forecaster. If the fresh sheets of stamps began to curl, it was sure to rain!

George Truelove, of Austwick, was a grocer for over 60 years. In the old days, he also had a horse and trap available for private hire. He stands behind his brass scales, surrounded by a host of commodities.

The village shop-cum-post office at Thoralby, in Bishopdale. Items on sale include tomatoes and pork pies, brushes and braces. As in the previous photograph, brass scales dominate the counter.

A contrast in shops. Those shown above were part of a group contained in a large wooden building erected when Bradford was building its reservoir at Scar House, head of Nidderdale. Falshaw is an old Wharfedale name, and the Buckden shop of James Falshaw has a signboard hinting at the range of goods and services to be found within. Petrol and motor oils were available; the glass-fronted collection of local view cards was of the type to be seen on the wall of many a Dales village shop.

Transport Without Wheels

THINK OF A SLEDGE, and a snowy landscape usually comes to mind. Yet in the upper dales, a sled could be used throughout the year. Drawn by a horse, it moved smoothly over the short, springy grasses of the upland fields.

The photographs in this section show the sled being used for a variety of purposes. In addition, it was employed, with a suitable body, for muck-spreading. The muck was collected at the middens near the field barns and deposited from the sled in heaps, which then were scaled to give the field an even covering of this important fertiliser. Making a sled was a combined operation by the local joiner and blacksmith, and maintenance costs were negligible.

Steep-sided valleys like Garsdale were perfectly suited to the use of sleds. Pictured on the left is a Garsdale farmer bringing back to the farm a load of bracken. The horse draws the sled easily. The sled itself has disappeared from sight under an immense mound of bracken, which was to be used as bedding for the stock in winter. Bracken was mown by scythe when it had died back in the autumn.

A most unusual sled is seen on the picture displayed on the next page. Basically, it is a hay sled, used at a farm at Thwaite, in Swaledale. The farmer had provided a superstructure to convert it into part pram, part sedan chair!

Pictured on the left is a haytime scene at Hebden, Wharfedale, that might have been taken in Victorian times. Showing a pony being used by Mr. Joy, it was photographed in 1940. The hayfield picture shown below was taken at Appersett, near Hawes, in Wensleydale. The study on the right is from Keld, Upper Swaledale; the farmer was portrayed as he collected a sick sheep for attention.

Church and Chapel

WITHIN LIVING MEMORY, nearly everyone in the Dales attended church or chapel on Sunday. For some families, attendance meant a walk of several miles, in all weathers. Although the church had witnessed in the Dales for centuries, families living in the remoter areas were to be more strongly influenced by Nonconformity. There is a profusion of little chapels.

The Friends established Meeting Houses, the old Independents had their chapels, the Inghamites once had a number of chapels, and the Methodists — both Primitives and Wesleyans — eventually attained numerical ascendancy.

On the opposite page, we see an Anglican procession in the ruins of Jervaulx Abbey, Wensleydale. Typical of the unpretentious churches serving a scattered farming community is Lunds, near the source of the river Ure. The Methodist chapel of Victorian days was simply furnished, with (invariably) a Scriptural text on the wall behind the pulpit. This photograph was taken at Keasden.

Chapel services were noted for the robust and homely messages of local preachers, revival meetings which became most fervent, and lusty hymn-singing, with the musical accompaniment provided by the harmonium. Among the mid-week gatherings were prayer meetings of great length and intensity.

Horse-power in the Dales

THE HORSE WAS MASTER of the dusty, waterbound roads. In summer, you could easily tell when a horse and cart were approaching by the cloud of lime dust. Every farmer had his horse or, in the upper dales, a "miniature cart horse", the Dales pony — a lively animal that was at home between shafts.

Shepherds in the Dales took out hay to their sheep in winter using a horse, with a sack of hay on either side, a task known as "jagging". The many tradesmen, doctors and veterinary surgeons, kept stables. A doctor usually employed a man to attend to his horse and vehicle, for someone must hold the horse while he visited his patients.

The boy with the horse (left) clearly has an awesome respect for his task of holding it. It is related that when a Dales farmer moved to another farm, some 20 miles from his old home, the only horse available was a mare, with foal at foot. The mare was harnessed to the cart which drew his belongings, and made journeys between the farms on several days, with the foal trotting blithely beside her.

The blacksmith was the "kingpin" of a rural community. A farmer with a horse only partly broken in for work might send it to the blacksmith, observing to his friends: "Yon hoss'll be brokken in reight by time t'smith's finished wi' it!" The photograph (left) shows an old-time blacksmith at Clapham, in North Craven.

In winter, the shoes worn by working horses were removed by the blacksmith and "frost-sharpened", so that an animal could maintain its balance on a slippery surface.

How the letters were delivered to Bolton Abbey when the King was in residence for grouse-shooting, as the chief guest of the Duke of Devonshire. This photograph dates from about 1912.

The smithy in the main street at Hawes, in Wensleydale, was for many years a scene of furious activity. The smith not only attended to horses; he also made and maintained a variety of implements and machines. There is a double-horse mower on the picture above. One of his most demanding tasks was fitting shoes to the feet of ponies brought unbroken from the fells. A Dales blacksmith described the operation as "blood for money." A smith also acted as a vet. When sharp "wolf" teeth formed behind a horse's grinders, he knocked out the "wolf" teeth by hammer and chisel!

A sight to excite a spectator was a large team of horses drawing recently-felled timber. It is believed that this photograph was taken near the village of Clapham.

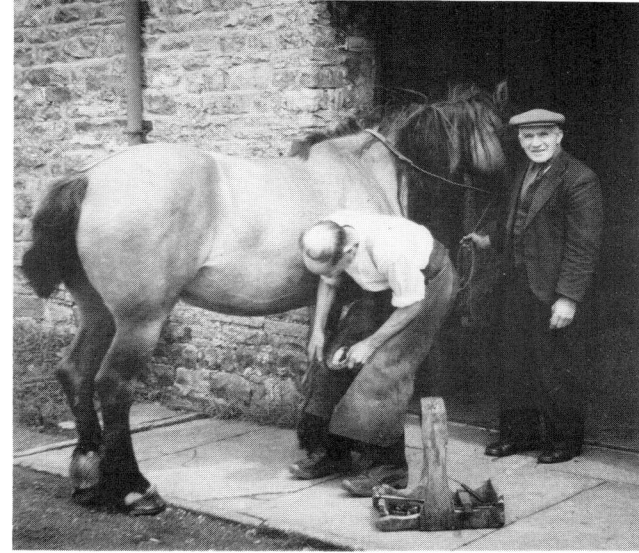

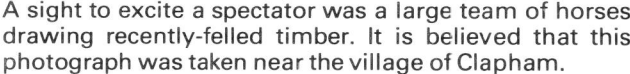

The blacksmith at work above had his business in Arkengarthdale, an off-shoot valley of Swaledale. Notice the traditional leathern apron and clogs. The busiest season in the upper dales was just before haytime. On the picture (left), the venerable-looking smith at Hebden looks with some suspicion towards the camera. The wooden wheel beside the building had doubtless been hooped by this smith and his helpers.

Milking Time

THE DALESMAN'S COW was the Shorthorn, which has now been supplanted by the Friesian. The Shorthorn served the domestic needs of a Dales family, and also yielded milk for conversion into butter and cheese — thence into cash — before large quantities of milk were despatched from the farms as milk, to be processed in distant dairies.

It was once customary to milk cattle out-of-doors in summer. The milk was transported to the farmhouse in a back-can, one of the two objects pictured above. The old photograph (above, left) shows Bryan Cockburn — in his Sunday suit — returning from milking with his cousin near Bainbridge in 1904. Some milkers strapped their back-cans on to motor bikes and drove to the summer pastures. An Angram man milked in a field beside the Buttertubs Pass, and an old chap from Keld drove his motor bike to a pasture high on Kisdon.

In the 1930s, a Wensleydale farmer "got eight gallons o' milk, put it on my back, and selt it for 5d a gallon. I was better off than t'chaps in Coverdale; they sent their milk to a firm who paid 'em only 4½d a gallon." The cattle soon became accustomed to being milked out-of-doors. A handful of special feed in a bucket encouraged them to drop their milk. "I'd milk one, then turn to see an owd lass standing patiently, watching t'bucket, wi' slather running over her chin."

Above: Hand-milking into a pail, near Ramsgill in Nidderdale. The picture (top, right) of a farmer driving in cows was also taken near Ramsgill. The most celebrated Shorthorn was the Craven Heifer (right).

Wensleydale Cheese

FOR CENTURIES a farmhouse occupation, cheese-making was eventually concentrated in factories. There is a creamery at Hawes where Wensleydale cheese, the best known of several varieties, is still produced.

In the old days, herds of cattle were small in size. Dalesfolk used up any surplus milk, as already related, in the making of butter or cheese. The cheese-making was mainly in the late spring and summer.

In the cheese was locked up the flavour of those old herby fields we knew before the land was ploughed and re-seeded with modern commercial strains of grass. "When you put milk in bowls, to separate the cream, you knew it was ready when the cream would 'od a penny."

Pictured above is Lane House, in Bishopdale, the barn bearing a sign "Wensleydale Cheese." A 17th century Wensleydale cheese press at Askrigg is also shown.

Mixing — a photograph taken at the creamery at Hawes. Factory production of cheese in this town at the head of Wensleydale began towards the end of last century.

Some Dales Communities

THOUGH STILL RECOGNISABLE to returning exiles, our Dales towns and villages have suffered many minor changes. On the opposite page is pictured a group of shawled women, presumably mill-workers, trudging through snow at Settle, in North Ribblesdale; and a general view of Reeth, in Swaledale, as it was some 30 years ago.

The old hall (above) was a prominent feature at Askrigg, in Wensleydale, until the building was destroyed by fire in the 1930s. The inn (top, right) stood near Semerwater, and is shown as it was in 1904. Old Sedbergh is portrayed on the right, and below is a photograph from Arncliffe featuring cyclists.

A World of Grey Stone

THE SHEEP FRAMED by roughly-hewn stone (left) was peering into the old church near Semerwater. Pictured above is a former thatched barn standing near Hurst, in Swaledale. The steep pitch of the gable end hints at its thatched state. Gap-walling was a continuing operation on the Dales farms. Many gaps occurred with the thaw after a hard snap. The two men on our photograph (right) were working at Halton Gill, in Littondale.

Driving Sheep

VARIOUS WAYS of driving sheep from place to place are shown in these photographs. On the left, sheep are seen passing through Rathmell, in Ribblesdale, and (below) a flock has just crossed the old bridge at Malham. On the right, a farmer in a van lets his dog do the work on the high road between Swaledale and Mallerstang. The mounted shepherd (below) was seen above Teesdale, and the farmer on the right was driving sheep near Calton, above Malhamdale.

Above: A device attached to the neck of a hill sheep is designed to stop if from breaking out of the field.
Right: Springtime near Keld, in Swaledale.

Fairs and Markets

The photograph is of hiring day at Hawes. The first two market days in July saw the congregation of men, often Irishmen, needing haytime employment on the farms. They reached mutually satisfying terms with local farmers. Many were anxious that they should have a good "bait (food) shop."

Two Wensleydale towns on market day. On the right is a packed market place at Leyburn. Laid out in the foreground are shovels and forks. Pictured above is Hawes, at the moment when some Shorthorn cattle were being driven down the street towards the auction mart.

Sheep sale at Kilnsey, in Wharfedale, in 1933. The auctioneer is Tom Taylor.

Arthur and John Taylor at Kilnsey, also in 1933. The sale took place in September.

The moment a purchase was made at Leyburn market.

Auction Mart at Hawes. *Right:* At Malham.

The Lighter Side of Dales Life

NOT LONG AFTER the snow has melted on Tan Hill, farmers gather for a show of Swaledale sheep. Clusters of farmers, from remote farms, also take the opportunity of catching up on the gossip since last they met in the previous autumn. The sale has never been a solemn occasion. The event — held near the famous isolated inn — is enlivened by the strains from a brass band.

Shortly after the 1914-18 war, folk dancing became popular, and outdoor demonstrations were arranged. Lilian Douglas, of Austwick, recorded some of the old dances of the Yorkshire Dales following conversations with old men who remembered them. The group on the right was at Gisburn, in Ribblesdale. On the far right is shown players at a ladies cricket match held at Settle in 1907. The hunting group, pictured outside the Wilson Arms Hotel at Threshfield, in Wharfedale, was from the Pendle Harriers.

Such events have been supplemented by a host of village shows and special occasions. In winter, whist drives and dances have always been popular. No occasion was missed to relieve the stresses of the long, dark nights.

HARDROW SCAR, HAWES, NORTH YORKSHIRE.

The Committee have pleasure in announcing to the Public, that (by the kind permission of the Right Honorable the Earl of Wharncliffe) they have made arrangements for holding their FIFTH ANNUAL

BRASS BAND & GLEE CONTEST

and

GRAND GALA

In Hardrow Scar Grounds,

On SATURDAY, JUNE 27TH, 1885,

WHEN PRIZES TO THE VALUE OF

£42 and £17

FOR BRASS BANDS   FOR GLEE SINGING

WILL BE OFFERED FOR COMPETITION.

AT THE CLOSE OF THE CONTEST, AN EFFICIENT QUADRILLE BAND WILL PLAY FOR

☛ DANCING ☚

WHICH WILL BE CONTINUED UNTIL EIGHT O'CLOCK.

In Hardrow Scar Grounds there is a

MAGNIFICENT WATERFALL

Situate at the extremity of a deep, narrow, rocky Glen, along which the stream winds amongst detached masses of rock; an immense Column of Water ONE HUNDRED FEET HIGH being projected from the edge of a rock, so as to detach itself completely from the strata beneath, and plunge without dispersion or interruption into a black and boiling cauldron below. The Cataract is thrown forward in such a manner that a good carriage road might be made behind the Fall, in consequence of the action of the air having decomposed the shale underlying the grit and limestone. The Grounds are laid out with extensive walks, and contain several other beautiful Cascades.

EXCURSION TRAINS

Will run from LEEDS BRADFORD COLNE and CARLISLE on the Midland Railway, and EAST and WEST HARTLEPOOL SOUTH BANK MIDDLESBROUGH NORTH STOCKTON and DARLINGTON on the North Eastern Railway, calling at Intermediate Stations. For times of starting &c. see Railway Companies' Bills.

ADMISSION: ONE SHILLING EACH.

REFRESHMENTS WILL BE PROVIDED ON THE GROUND.

C. H. RICHARDSON, Esq. President; J. W. FRYER, Esq. Treasurer; EDWARD MOORE, Secretary.

PRINTED BY THOS. HODGES, WENSLEYDALE PRINTING WORKS, HAWES.

ALMOST EVERY little community had its brass band. The highlight of the year was the annual contest at Hardraw, in Upper Wensleydale, where a bandstand (shown above) was erected in the narrow valley below the famous waterfall. Seen on the opposite page (top, left) is the Bainbridge Band, of Wensleydale, mustered on this occasion to help celebrate the Coronation of Edward VII. Below it are seen members of the band at Gunnerside, in Swaledale.

Fiddle and accordian were used to provide the music at an old Maytime gathering at Linton, in Wharfedale, as shown in the picture (far right). Both were employed to tuneful effect at the Dales dances. Dancing was not restricted to public halls. It was not uncommon in winter for friends to gather for a social evening. Many a set of Lancers has been danced on the flagged floor of a farmhouse kitchen.

A Dales Haytime

OUR PHOTOGRAPH of a farmer near Dent (above) immediately suggests that there has been a good haytime. He is cheerful. A good crop is vital. This is the fodder for cattle and sheep during the long winter. Farmers hope to have at least half the hay remaining in their barns in mid-February, for not until May are cattle turned out to graze.

The Dales farmer is "keyed up" at the approach of haytime. Do not try to engage him in conversation. Agree with everything he says, or he may "snap your head off." In poor weather, he is thoroughly depressed, yet when the good weather arrives he is a superman, mustering enough strength and spirit to manage on little more than four hours' sleep a night for 10 days, maybe even a fortnight. In the old days, before machines, haytime was reckoned to last about a month.

Given good weather, clearing a field was classically a three-day operation: the grass was cut one day, turned the next and gathered as hay on the third. Some farmers sledded their hay to the barn; others employed horse and cart, the cart having the addition of "shelvings" to increase its carrying capacity. In "chancy" weather, it was necessary to secure the hay against rain, and this was done by making small, well-packed heaps, the tops of which would turn the weather. The basic heap was known as the "foot-cock". A much larger heap (the "pike") was made to secure the hay for a longer period and, indeed, some farmers piked most of the hay in the fields and then led the hay from pike to barn.

Refreshing drinks were provided for the helpers. Ginger beer stood in stone bottles. Nettle beer was produced; it was cheap. A lemon drink — with real lemons, not "extract" — was frequently made by the farmers' wives for the haytime men and, of course, there was a barrel of ale for the Irish helpers.

The reek of tractor exhaust fumes hangs over the meadow where, in days within living memory, nearly every operation was performed by hand. Men and women, holding wooden rakes, worked rhythmically along the swathes and turned them. Hay was hand-forked on to the cart, and later from cart to barn. In those quieter days, the corncrakes could nest in peace. Their rasping call from the meadows was a distinctive sound of a Pennine haytime.

A two-horse mowing machine being used in Craven.

"Strawing" hay with a single-horse machine in Craven.

John Coates rakes hay on land between Penyghent and Fountains Fell. The farm, Rainscar, is set over 1,000 feet above sea level.

The Middletons, of Deepdale, working in a meadow at an elevation of 800 feet above sea level. The family is using rakes to turn the hay. Machines now perform this ancient occupation.

Late July, at Dent Head Farm. The rakings from a large meadow are stacked on a horse-drawn sled for transportation to the barn. The sled was commonly used in steep meadows. Its iron-shod runners moved easily over grass.

Opposite page, top: Haytime near Ingleborough.
Bottom: A hay sweep at a farm in Teesdale. *Above, left:*
A creel used for carrying hay in Wensleydale. *Left:* Single
horse mowing machine, Cathole near Sedbergh. *Above:*
This tithe barn at Wigglesworth, in Ribblesdale, was
seriously damaged by fire.

The "Lead Dales"

QUIET GILLS leading off the northern dales, and moorland between Wharfedale and Nidderdale, are pock-marked by the spoil heaps from lead mines. The industry had faded by the close of last century, but the memories linger on.

In Gunnerside Gill (left) is prominent evidence of lead-mining. In the picture we look across the gill from stonework, in which a water-wheel was set, to a spoil heap on which stands a building, part of which was used as a blacksmith's shop. Pictured on the next page are what remained — some years ago — of an old lead smelt mill in Arkengarthdale. Below this picture can be seen a pair of lead-miners' boots.

Miners talked endlessly about such aspects of mining as trials (exploratory workings) and flats (the horizontal ore deposits), adits (drainage tunnels) and the bouse itself (which was unwashed ore). They spoke with some reverence about t'Owd Man, their name both for the miners of yesteryear and the old workings into which they periodically broke. T'Owd Man's enterprise, his shrewdness and industry, at a time before technological improvements had transformed the industry, were topics of awed contemplation wherever miners met.

By and large, the miners were grave, reflective men; they did not fritter away on such pleasures as strong drink the money they had hard-earned. They rarely used bad language, for many of them were devout Methodists. Last century, a Mr. Forster wrote: "The lead-miners are remarkably intelligent and well educated. There are books in almost every cottage. Attendance at public worship is the rule, not the exception, and profane language is scarcely ever heard."

By the time the industry declined, being unable to compete successfully with importations of inexpensive lead from overseas, most of the important veins had been picked clean. Many families had to leave the Dales — for either the industrialised North-East or the Lancashire cotton towns.

Lead-miners at work, Greenhow Hill (between Wharfedale and Nidderdale) in the 1920s.

Reek of Petrol

THE INVASION of the Dales by visitors anxious to enjoy the exceptional scenery was given a boost by the development of motor vehicles. Many families now had high mobility. Pictured above is a sign put up by a motoring enthusiast at Clapham to warn fellow motorists of police traps ahead; it dates from 1903. A little earlier, the road up Buckhaw Brow had been as portrayed above — a strip of road with a loose surface, which was puddly in wet weather and a-swirl with dust in dry conditions.

Yet by the early 1920s, a photographer could record a scene such as that on the opposite page — an assembly of cars and motor-cycles on the green at Burnsall, in Wharfedale. Notice, on the right, three impressive charabancs — big open buses, with a door to each row of seats and a canvas hood that was erected if it began to rain. Such vehicles brought a day's trip to the Dales within reach of people with modest means. A charabanc might be hired by, say, a West Riding church choir for its annual outing.

Right: A Wharfedale bus at Burnsall in about 1907.
Below: Congestion on the green at Burnsall as visitors take advantage of unrestricted parking on turf by the river. Even the dalesfolk showed interest in such an assembly of sparkling vehicles.

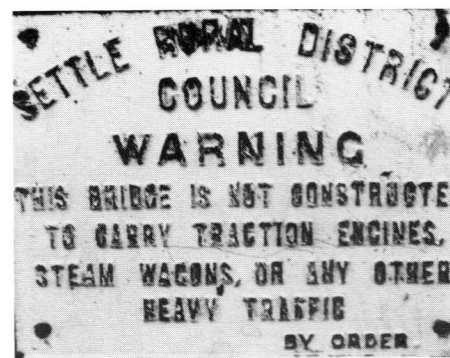

SETTLE RURAL DISTRICT
COUNCIL
WARNING
THIS BRIDGE IS NOT CONSTRUCTED
TO CARRY TRACTION ENGINES,
STEAM WAGONS, OR ANY OTHER
HEAVY TRAFFIC
BY ORDER

Left: Ted Harrison, who was employed by the Farrers of Clapham, with one of the first motor cars to be seen in Craven. *Above:* Sign on a bridge in North Craven. *Below:* An early tourer in the Craven limestone country.

The West Yorkshire Garage, at Settle (above) was established early in the motoring story to cater for the needs of enthusiasts in North Ribblesdale. Pictured on the left is the first motor bus to run in the Dales. Laycocks, of Cowling, had vehicles at an earlier date, but the bus on this photograph operated between Skipton and Buckden. It was here photographed outside the Temperance Hotel, at Grassington, in the summer of 1908. Its driver, H. Kirkley, was killed during the 1914-18 war.

Above: Scene at Dibbles Bridge, between Hebden and Greenhow, when a motor coach came to grief in 1925. *Left:* a motorcycle trial at Keighley Gate, above Ilkley, Wharfedale. The machine with a sidecar is a Scott, manufactured at nearby Bradford.

A Dalesman and his Dog

SHEEP FARMING is made possible on the vast upland grazings of the Dales largely because in the collie dog the farmer has a speedy means of rounding up his stock, as for dipping or in advance of a blizzard. The farmer uses four main whistles of command: the "stop" whistle and "come on" whistle, used whether the dog is moving towards its owner or is driving the sheep away, and the two "flank" whistles, instructing the animal to turn left or right. The orthodox words of command for the flank movements are "Come by" (go left) and "Away here" (right).

A Dales shepherd and his dog, which must deal firmly but not viciously with the sheep.

Where a public road crosses a common on which sheep are grazed, some sheep are inclined to wander off the open ground along stretches of road flanked by walls. Today, cattle grids prevent such truancy, but there was a time when some farmers put dogs on sentry duty. They occupied a small kennel on the edge of the common, and were tied to it by a chain. Their excited barking, and quick movements, discouraged any nomadic sheep.

Two collie dogs, photographed at a sheep dog trial. Some events call for "double-dogging". Working two dogs simultaneously is a skilful task. Remember that when two dogs are used, there must also be two distinct sets of commands to avoid confusion.

Tups and Yows

THE PHOTOGRAPH (right) was taken in a bleak countryside where the Swaledale type of sheep is thoroughly at home. The croft stands beside the Buttertubs Pass. Here sheep are being temporarily penned while the farmer attends to them.

The male sheep is called a tup, tip or ram. The head of a fine Swaledale tup was used as the emblem for the Yorkshire Dales National Park. A female is a ewe, or yow. A hostelry in Upper Wharfedale used the sheep terms as notices on the doors of some outside toilets, to the confusion of visitors from towns who were not familiar with sheep.

The Dales have been pastoral country since the coming of the Norse settlers about 1,000 years ago. The sheep ensure that the landsape remains open, almost devoid of trees, for the animals graze incessantly, preventing natural regeneration of timber. Up to 70 inches of rain a year may fall on the fleeces of the sheep. The ewes carry their lambs through the worst weeks of the year, when snow lies on the felltops and the crags are sheathed by ice.

The Swaledale sheep originated on and around Tan Hill. Farmers decided on a type that suited them, and bred to that type. The Swaledale, best suited to moist ground, has spread far and wide. Many large flocks are now found in Cumbria and on North-Eastern moors. In the Craven area, the sheep breed favoured is the Dalesbred. Farmers on the slaty fells around Sedbergh breed a type of sheep known as a Rough Fell.

A Dalesbred ewe and its lamb, photographed in the Clapham district.

Two collie dogs turning a sheep. One has approached too closely. The farmer shouts "Leave it."

Frank Beresford, Scale Farm, Horton-in-Rbblesdale, attends to a ewe and its new lamb.

Above: A line-up of Swaledale tups at the Tan Hill Show.
Below: The Campbells, father and son, of Horton-in-Ribblesdale, with two prize Dalesbreds.

Sheep are normally timid creatures, not easily approached. There are two exceptions: in February and March, which is "starvation time" on the hills, and the sheep are sometimes frantic for food; and at the shows, when sheep are penned and can be closely approached. A prize tup that is handled too much can become jaded, but a few days back on the hills soon restores to it clear eyes and a lost vitality.

A fine Swaledale tup is pictured above. Notice the dark head and grey muzzle. By providing such sheep with horns, nature has given the farmer ideal "handles" to hold when he wishes to restrain a tup!

Hand-shearing Dales sheep. *Above:* Mr. H. Plews, of West Scale Park, Kettlewell, neatly strips an animal of its jacket. *Top, right:* The Handleys, clipping a tup at Cautley. A Rough Fell is a hefty animal, and two men were sometimes needed to do this work. *Right:* Farmer Metcalfe clips a "straggler" at a fold above Muker, in Swaledale.

Sheep-clipping at Raisgill Farm, Yockenthwaite. The "catcher" returns to the fold to collect more sheep. Most of the animals are being clipped on the ground. The man on the left of the photographer is winding a fleece.

A SUNNY DAY, near the Wainwath Falls, in Upper Swaledale. A batch of Swaledale sheep is penned to await the clipping. The man on the left has an ingenious "stock". A plank has been positioned with one end over a bar of the fencing and the other end supported by a wooden stool. The farmer on the right clips his sheep on the ground. In the old days, sheep were "salved" in November. A mixture of grease and tar was applied to the skin, the wool having been hand-shedded. The last traces of the salve were removed by washing in the local beck, about a fortnight before the time appointed for clipping.

Sheep-clipping by hand at Ribblehead, in the 1930s. The older type of farmer preferred to clip his sheep on a "stock", a form of wooden bench.

Kilnsey Crag, in Wharfedale, looks out over large, flat fields to the river. These big fields are used annually for the agricultural show. On the day this photograph was taken, a sheep sale was planned. The farmer — and his alert collie dog — were driving a flock of young sheep updale beside the village of Kilnsey, and into the shadow of the famous Crag.

Dalesfolk — by Adoption

A NUMBER OF MEN who were not born in the Dales have achieved distinction through their association with the region. On the left is Halliwell Sutcliffe, novelist, and author of a Dales classic, "The Striding Dales." Thomas Armstrong (above) settled near Low Row, in Swaledale. He was noted for the intense and prolonged research he undertook into a subject before writing a novel based upon it. His study of lead-mining led to the publication of "Adam Brunskill". On the opposite page are portrayed Arthur Raistrick, a prolific writer on scientific and historical aspects of the Dales, and Fred Lawson, of Castle Bolton, who visited Wensleydale on a holiday — and decided to stay. He is well remembered as a great artist.

Walter Morrison, of Malham Tarn House, which he called his "mountain home." He presented the domed chapel to Giggleswick School.

The Dales in Carnival Mood

HORNER, photographer of Settle, was present when a fair was set up in the market place of the old Ribblesdale town (left). Such a fair was thoroughly enjoyed by people at a time when there was little spare money and work occupied almost every waking hour.

On this page are presented two pictures taken at an annual festivity held at West Witton, near Leyburn. In the late evening, a procession down the village is led by two men who carry a life-size effigy of Old Bartle (believed to be a corruption of Bartholomew, who is the patron saint of the local church). Stops are made, ancient words are intoned, and in due course the effigy is burnt to the accompaniment of old songs. There is much speculation about the custom. Some people have it that it dates to the time of the Reformation, when fanatics seized an image of St. Bartholomew from the church and burned it.

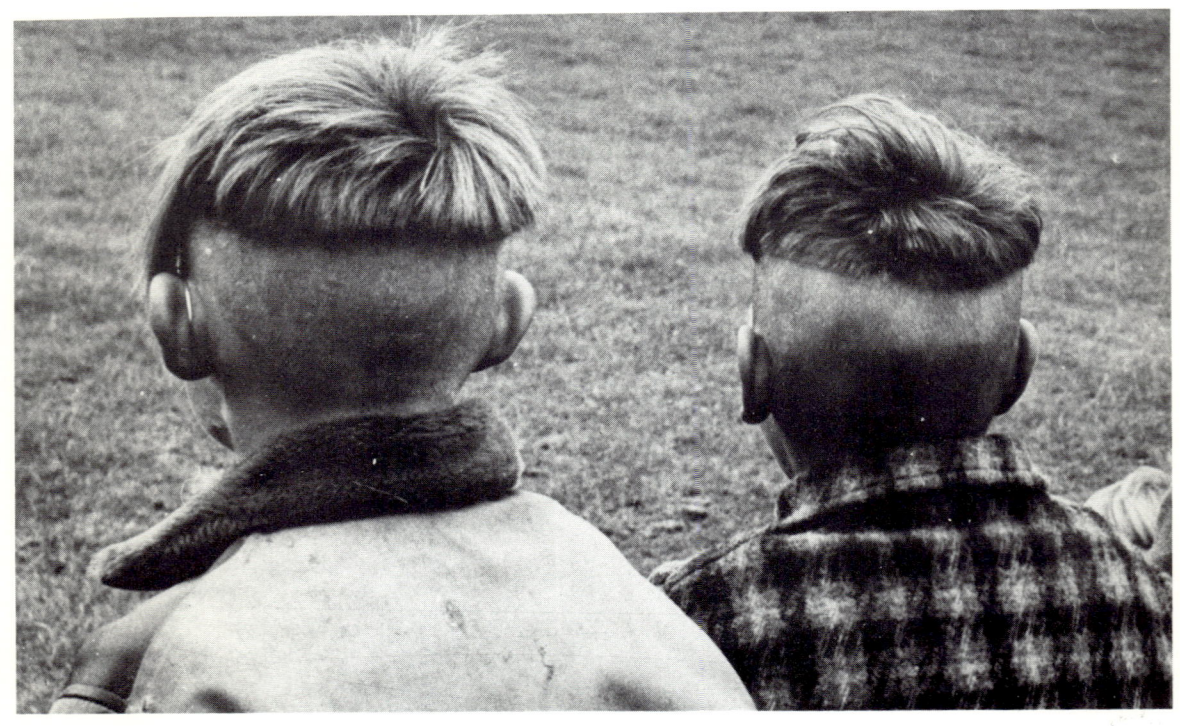

The long and the short. "Pudding basin haircuts", photographed at an agricultural show in Wensleydale. Was a pudding basin used for this style, or did father employ his sheep shears?

Outside back cover: On tow—a variety of vehicles on the main road at Giggleswick, looking towards the Mains.